ABSENCE,
LUMINESCENT

ABSENCE, LUMINESCENT

Valerie Martínez

FOUR WAY BOOKS
Marshfield

Four Way Books
PO Box 607
Marshfield, MA 02050

Library of Congress Catalogue Card Number: 98-72338

ISBN 1-884800-23-8

Cover art, cover and text design: The Creative Team
Four Way Books is a division of Friends of Writers, Inc.,
a Vermont-based not-for-profit organization. Publication
of this book was made possible by generous support
from individual donors.

Acknowledgments

I would like to acknowledge the following publications where these
poems, or versions of them, have appeared:

The Best American Poetry, 1996: "It Is Not"
The Bloomsbury Review: "Pastorale"
Confluence: "Into the Next One," "Coastal," "Meridian"
Parnassus: "Night of Fathers"
Permafrost: "Infinite," "The Annunciation," "On Absence"
Prairie Schooner: "Absence, Luminescent," "Nocturne," "Tesoro,"
"Outside: Winter Solstice," "Prayer," "It Is Not"
Puerto del Sol: "And Seeing It"
Rhetoric Review: "Geode," "Savor, Harvest"
Riverrun: "The Little Number"
Touching the Fire: Fifteen Poets of Today's Latino Renaissance:
"Absence, Luminescent," "It Is Not," "Nocturne," "Tesoro,"
"Night of Fathers," "The New World," "The Reliquaries,"
"Children of the Disappeared," "Traveler," "The Human Universe"

Publication of this book
was supported by a generous grant
from the Greenwall Fund
of the Academy of American Poets.

for Ramón and Exilda
siempre, de un amor profundo

CONTENTS

I've come upon the boats.
Surround me like islands, bodies.
Choose. Cannot. Gather
my provisions. Kiss darkness, light.
The path to my vessel—
dreamlike, forget.
How everything converges on it.

Part One:

The Territories of Absence

THE LITTLE NUMBER

*A cell, in Beijing Prison #1, reserved
for political prisoners. Only as large
as a cardboard box, its light is never
turned off.*

How I dream, it opens:
        I have the bruised legs of that girl
                with baskets, soft peaches
for my mouth. She never sits.
        Her hair keeps falling, sticking
                to her white teeth.

Awake, with the bulb on and on.
        Get one breath out, one in,
                before the room closes.
View of my limbs over and over. No thing
        comes back, no remember
                inside the little number.
It's my own voice, closest, with the light
        on and on. I haven't spoken.
        Write the walls
with my eyes. Press the walls out.
        Logic of walls with their numerics,
                angles, borders—

Forest: it's the soul of the girl
        feeding me. It's the soul
                of the girl in my mouth.
I'm not myself, too close.
        It's another man's knees pulled up,
                sores on the bones, sitting.
His spine with its islands of dark bruises.
        I swallow it.
                He confesses anything.

IT IS NOT

We have the body of a woman, an arch over the ground, but there is no danger. Her hair falls, spine bowed, but no one is with her. The desert, yes, with its cacti, bursage, sidewinders. She is not in danger. If we notice, there are the tracks of animals moving east toward the sunrise. And the light is about to touch a woman's body without possession. Here, there are no girl's bones in the earth, marked with violence. A cholla blooms, just two feet away. It blooms.

There is a man, like her father, who wakes to a note saying *I have gone, for a day, to the desert.* Now he knows she is in danger. He will try to anticipate what happens to a young woman, how it will happen, how he will deal with the terrible. In him, he feels he knows this somehow. He knows because there are men he knows who are capable. This place she has gone to, where? But it doesn't matter. There is, first of all, the heat which scorches, snakes with their coils and open mouths, men who go there with the very thing in mind. The very thing.

It is the desert on its own. Miles. Beyond what anyone can see. Not peaceful nor vengeful. It does not bow down. It is not danger. I cannot speak of it without easing or troubling myself. It is not panorama nor theatre. I do not know. It is conception—the gifts or burdens I bear, whether arch, a prayer, or danger. They can happen, yes, we conceive them. This very woman I know. The man does sit tortured. The desert, created, merely embodies its place. And watch us lay our visions, O god, upon it.

BLACK OUT

Taken with the urban, the sky
downs the streetlights like a hurricane.
Something failed in the long wires
holding the houses up.

They always talk during the news.
No news or lights or images
tearing at the borders of things.
So dark they want to use their teeth.

The looters sound wild in the streets
and they think they hear tanks rolling in.
Darkness of occupation? Imagination?
No voice with word from the outside.
Locked in.

A coup for the ham radio operator.
Hears the fragments of heroism and violence
with headphones on. No witness
to the girl in a car, stalled
at the outskirts. No girl.

How to navigate in this world?
Map the territories of absence.
The Prime Minister of Messages
taps out a tune in the dark.
In a view of the world without light.

Is it gunshot? Firework snap?

How to function in the night,
no sleep, no dreams.
Marking the boundaries
like troops and tanks.
Some other country.

Kiss violently, send out images
of yourself, fraidy cats.

SAVOR, HARVEST

I wake from a dream of animals
and remember the painting
where the angel tells Mary
and each word's painted gold
from his mouth to hers.
Sometimes it's all in the dark
or through the eyes.

I get up and think of swans
and fat owls differently.
And the painting,
the message still speaks to me:
sometimes I want words painted
from my mouth to yours.

Today I'll see things like Giotto did—
just more than two-dimensional.
Nothing more beautiful than that
some days, then darkness.

There's something to preparing
ourselves for sleep. As a child,
I buried my animals properly.
So what's the creature to us?
I have my midnight rituals,
the animal body I take
and sleep so deep
that pictures come out of me.

AND SEEING IT

Orange, orange. And the hand arching up
to hold it. The woman's hand. The arching.
Up. And the star exploding, seeing it
where it wasn't, a telescope on the night sky.
The thermonuclear flash.
The explosion.

She had her hand out; it fell
like an explosion into her fingers.
It wasn't the scope and the eye,
was hand, fruit. It was what I saw.
It was what I imagine I somehow saw.

Out on the horizon of stars beyond the gigantic sun.
Beyond the measure of the sun the star bursting.

And it was autumn. The shadows of oleanders
made colors of bodies on the lawn.
The girls' dresses were red on the green lawn.
Smelling of fruit.
Making shapes of fruit in their hands.

With the sky all opaque, and the one star.

There, at the top of the fingers, the orange.
At the tip like God and Adam touching.
Like the ceiling of the Sistine where the stars might be.

And knowing about hydrogen, carbon.
A collapsing in. The water drunk by girls,
the breath given out. Breath, out.

The table of elements, the elements served up.
Iron in the spinach in the aqua bowl.
Green explosion in the aqua bowl.

Clusters of grape stems without grapes.
Molecular models like grape stems.
To what we address, link.
To what we speak.

Not in our lifetime will we see it.
Not in the sky like this: supernova.
Not ever again they say.
Drops. The orange.

NIGHT OF FATHERS

"I have come at the wish of my heart from the pool
of Double Fire...Give to me my mouth [that] I may
speak with it. May I follow my heart at its season of
fire and night."

From *The Egyptian Book of the Dead*

Like a wavering gem, floating,
  the tethers holding me
over the fields of ill, farewell.
  Toward the region beyond, gone

out of my body. No more heart,
  no thighs to shiver,
recesses of hurt. To the sun
  moving through corn and wheat.
The table with water and cakes.
  The elaborate feast we imagine.

And the limbs coming back, there,
  like the wished, small animals
come home. And the forms sorrow takes:
  winds, rains, the bursts of nature.
Reclaiming:

the red pump, all artery, chamber,
  the palms and wrists indented
with the shapes of new things.
  The inner thighs so sweet,
their little white marks.

And the forms the memory takes—
  dreams of iron weight, doves
flying in the belly, wings furious.
  Waters, waters, pools

at the horizon of eyes.

And the mouth given, flying back
   to the face, the last,
the dangerous, for see how it wants,
   it remembers. Curved bow
holds the shapes of sufferings,
   those fathers. And the lover's
weakness, places. Then plummeting

back to the lived. Mouth now
   emptied of lies must take us back
to the dwelling places:
   the hurt, earth, hurt beautiful.

MEAGEN'S FLUTE

The silverleaf oaks curve,
white trunks bending and crossing,
rising into pleaches against a sky
just going dark. We look down
from the ridge to a valley of green whorls
like pools of moss. And then sound,
lone as an infant's, or some turtledove
from behind. Time to sit on the rocks,
mute mosaics: rose, pale-green, green amber.
Reminded of something like prayer
in those who come to rest
on pilgrimage—take a moment to,
rapt in some devotion. Then,
we are moving into sound, crouched
like silent *o*'s in someone's mouth,
through which flute music will float.
In there just before music, a deaf moment,
then a note into air, O Sweet,
from Meagen's mouth to mountain air
and we are looking up to see the night
this violet, these velvet robes of song.

NOCTURNE

To the interior, limbs folded
(happens inside) the ankle bent
like weep. It is the body,
attitude of darkness,
eyes on the sorry, sorry.
Awake, so far away,
like a ghost.
And the song in the street,
distant trill, aria.
Some enormous pomp.
While the ravens shine on,
and all the streetlights.
While the scorpion holds
its anger—ready, ready.
In the eyes, once, the neck.
Bathed in green, turquoise, aquamarine, black.
Like the six scarves at the window.
The prism of scarves.
The mouth resting in the valley of nerves.
And how it turns: the teeth
just there, the windows
with their screens and bellows.
The word on the sharpest edge,
undoes, leaves.
And how the hands go, hold up,
filter the yellow, autumn night.
Find the sweet notes, sing
gone, gone, it's how, it's home.

CHILDREN OF THE DISAPPEARED

Argentina

The curved pelvic bone dug up,
showing childbirth before death.
The bullet hole near the top of the skull.

The boy misbehaves, arrives home
covered with petals and mud.
Unearthed from the neighbor's flower bed.
He gets the back of the hand several times.
She tells him he's a brat.
She tells him he's a burden
she can't bear. Later
she throws her delicate hairbrush
through a window of the house.
Her husband goes for her neck, for her hands.
She calls him a murderer
who shot the child's mother.
She can't tolerate the boy, won't
tolerate what isn't really hers any longer.
Better to be barren.

The boy's room is like a womb
with too many windows.
Half-awake, he lies on the good cheek
remembering the garden.
Hears *mother....longer.*
Sees white worms, petals in a pile of earth.
He is looking for treasures:
flint, animal bones, obsidian, iron.
A door slams. Someone—mother?—
is shouting somewhere.

He dreams the front door opening,
the porch superimposed on the flower bed,
spilling out. A woman he doesn't know
at the door, hand to mouth, calling
....*home now,*
come now,
find your way home.

PRAYER

for my father

From the home sky, these names:

> father, front yard, caterpillar, sun.

A force toward the house there,
forced to the house, the children come.

> (to the one who can't sleep)
> (to the one who wrings his hands, not sleeping)

Chiffon-green, the first caterpillar in the rosebed,
first thing. Who watches it, watches father

> (good sun, oxygen in the sun)

With the sky all pulled around, fastened to one place.
The elements called upon, selfishly, to one place.

> *(O great—the water—sun down—*
> *breath come—of the black earth—)*

And to the nightmarish mornings:
anxious, hopeless, powerless, lone.
To the page which suffers to name

> (the good medal, scapular, charm?)

Some trial some test some ill luck some barbarous feast

> And the body all crouched,
> the hair pushed, pulled out

From the questioning to the gods. From the landscape
seeming to turn away, turn off. From the witnessing,
the body made to witness. These things:

father, front yard, caterpillar, sun

toward healing.

Part Two:

From Stone to Diaphanous Silk

THE NEW WORLD

You are the kind of beauty
which delivers me up to some
midnight vision of water—
dark, enigmatic, moving
with figures so exotic
they must be ancient animals.
Somehow it happens
that the new world emerges
out of restlessness, the sleepless
turning of colors in darkness.
This is about love and not
insomnia, about belonging
and not the blackmares of evening.
The animals are gentle
as sweet mothers, bold
as fiesty amazons,
and there I am
looking like a pharaoh's queen,
abstract and beautiful.
I couldn't tell whether
I was asleep or waking,
but this came after a memory of you
slicing open a wild cucumber
to reveal the cool, orange pulp.
It was southern Africa, hot.
Your hair was cut too short,
like a boy's, and it was illegal
to play with nature by cutting.
But I wanted to see, wanted
even more than the rhinos
and newborn ostriches,
the young elephants up close.

It was blooming from the vine
like a drop of green water.
And nothing stopped you
from granting my wish,
nothing, nothing.
It was how much you wanted,
for my desire,
how many images
you've cut open,
O Love,
for me.

OUTSIDE: WINTER SOLSTICE

I bathe you with my robe open.
The heat rises from the floor
and moves our hair. Your skin
is nearly transparent in water.
It's morning, you close your eyes,
we've missed a thousand other details.

THE RELIQUARIES

Seaside, and the fragment of one running—
calves, ribs, green eyes into water.
There he goes. Waves. Buoying up
as into sky. And the seagulls fly,
seeing it as relief, a story. Once

they were there, two on a white blanket.
The circumference of a shadow.
Sunlight around that shadow.
The relation of two: bathers,
robed figures configured as one.
And she touches him—tender—and it is done.

(I've gone back to it. I've, I've—
it's not where I am. I give it away again.)
You're there. It's still in the sand.
It's trying to chisel it in.

How it comes forth: the story.
Wanting it, carving it down to vision.
Architecture, a coliseum of bent light,
the beautiful scatter of broken stones.
(And I can turn it into stones.)
Love, love: a portico, a labyrinth.

And his simple aquatics, legs and arms
in the brackish, etched against white fish.
The song, under there, of how he'll leave,
and naturally, like all living things:
animals, summer, daylight for the eves.

And the buildings, all shadows and beings:

block, angels, curves. With the love,
memory of all loves. The pediments,
these reliquaries.

It's our landscape, artifact—it might hurt.
(Run to, run away from it.)

ON ABSENCE

The military jets are making parabolic moves against the blue again. The sky's all cut out in pieces. It's so hot today, everything seems to bend back. No black widow on the porch anymore. She's left. And my hair is less dark, sunlit. Today I'll eat strawberries on the porch outside, with the sun through a glass of tea like a bullet. No rain. That bird cooing at my window at five a.m. No rain. Everything is detail and distance. The Chinese students laying their bodies down, rising up. The traffic skidding and speeding all night on Alvernon. Distance, because it defines us. And love held up to it, my prism. Is this the letter you wanted, all particulars, beauties, tortures? And just like those Japanese photos, black forms etched in an empty field: snow, cows, sea—by a lover's eye.

JUNE ELIXIR

The city's all mood and mischief,
   works its weight on me,
its detail, heat. While you admire
   the girl with the brunette heap,
big teeth. She's an urban oddity,
   beauty, in this dusty sunset
half-minute. Like a cool glass
   coming at us. It's summer
and we're wading like lovers
   on some island trip.
So much for love, and you're
   part of the pavement undulating
under pedestrians like me.
   I could kiss you under that cap
and it won't come close to the heat
   of the steering wheel, driving east
to the coffeehouse. Girls, lemonade,
   men with their t-shirts
cut to shreds. O, it sizzles!
   My castaway, offer me the oceans
of your neck—it's desert all over.
   For the sake of all this:
swoon and sweat my sweet.

MERIDIAN

A day of sun and clouds at the meridian
makes them half-aware. At the pelvis
the atmosphere stops. They're among
the plants they love, fir and thistle.
They can see the traces of others
in the woods, like handprints in clay.

What is their labor, effort? It's the clay
they love, on the mountain, the meridian
of what the earth gives at the pelvis
of the horizon. And here and there among
them in this, sweet spines, is the thistle.
Along with it, the memory of others.

In the city, they'd unwrapped for the others
an expensive mask—a little theatre in clay.
When they first heard someone say *meridian*
it seemed obvious—the mask was like a pelvis.
Gathering earth they don't talk among
themselves anymore, some silence for the thistle.

The mask accompanies them stuck with a thistle
in the mouth. They mark the absence of others.
At night, when the campfire's out, they mix clay
and touch—believe this is the meridian
of their years, and honor the pelvis,
lip, neck, collarbone they move among.

They smell snow from six months ago. Among
what illusions had they lived? A thistle
for the hemisphere of memory and others.
Regardless of day or hour, there is clay

in canvas bags. They sit in the sun's meridian
two days beyond plan, imagining a pelvis

hung next to the mask, and the pelvis
in both of them, its form. Among
which hands will it move, this thistle?
It is a souvenir, a storybook for others.
This time it wasn't only the sky and clay
that moved them to such a meridian.

Others would find them in a kiss at the meridian,
thistle-blown, sudden. One day the clay
pelvis rises from moving hands: undone, among.

MONSTROUS

Whoosh   the dancer/flame loops
lights him up   All the paper

twisting/burning How he walks
out   kisses/hisses her

Zozobra with the works   fire/
pinwheels all aflame with

What s/he sparked   ang/her
tend/her in him   Thousands

in the ballpark   watch
thousands   Calling him (back)

Old Man Gloom–about   to burn
The black go spirits away

go lover goodbye   to the clouds
of ghosts—sheets on the little ones

(in their tennis shoes)near   Gorgeous/
grotesque   these moans & wails

gesturegesture   The white
effigy/   the burn up

Seethemtimeagothe kissed—
the sacrifice (onetoanother)

and now   Goes the way/
suitcase   photo   bracelet.

One tin earring (this year)
on Zo   zobra/how his eyes

(giant pie tins) green glow
The when as adults we know

The when we didn't know
Magic! And all

the   midnights/flames
        monster/love.

BETWEEN SALVATION AND DESIRE

The summer after the season I left you, I built costumes for soldiers and gentlemen, for the diva in Kálmán's "Maritza." During the first week, my fingers were bloody, then the tips wore to callouses, somewhat dirty. And it was Salomé who hypnotized, writhing on stage in search of perfect love. In the next room, her costumes slowly emerged from paper to velvet and chiffon and at night you drifted strangely into them as my fingertips healed, idle, in sleep. She could not distinguish between salvation and desire—St. John's voice penetrating her every organ, divine fiber. She was delicate, sixteen, but what she'd learned from Herodius was the taste of lust and bitterness. It was the perfect love part that kept me going. I hadn't realized that violence is the lost child of affection. And not distinguishing between love and possession is the most dangerous. I left you. My hands bled over silk, muslin, linen, and the story mended them. Salomé made love to the severed head of St. John. You are left with my clothes, necklaces, gloves. How sweet your hands could be. How lost and wild and rough as I turned away.

ELEGY

for Ken Lang

Holding your spirit money
a girl descends
from a perch in the violet
air
In her gown she is a birthmark
sending you
on your way   With her
a phalanx
of Chinese screens: wings and
breezes and figurines
in the attitudes of farewell
And you
incense burning off in a silk
robe   All of you
counted   fanned   sweet
as white jade
heavenward turning
Where we
cannot see—

TESORO

for Timothy Trujillo
1951-1991

Just a few years ago, when everything was permanent.
Or on the edge of. Or, yes, perhaps over the edge,
or falling away from--

Was like the façades of the Sagrada Familia
with their delicate foliage, swans and turtles
bearing the weight of. Everything alive
& carved out of stone.

It was my treasure, this permanence,
the architecture of living. Everything
stone-true & buttressed: arc & arc & arc
of an ancient city.

Can you guess what will come next? Can you?
Touching you like the sheerest handkerchief
of silk? When the beloveds fell from the sky
& disappeared? From stone to diaphanous silk.
On the wind. Sudden.

It was a mistake, amiss. It was perception
of what is light as what is heavy & permanent.
Sometimes, one's hand can pass through stone,
& it is not a dream.

One got sick & another, another.
Someone I loved, who loved me,
disappeared. Two, or is it three,
who died. This is honest enough,

enough to say bluntly.
This is for Tim.

In *The Visitation* it is beautiful:
the handmaid's arms are barely covered,
tender skin beneath transparent silk.
The painter made no mistake,
the maiden is the most present of all.
She could be taken on the wind
with those invisible wings
& she is real, impermanent.
Her weight compares to no universe.

To hear it in my sleep—*tesoro*—
the hardest gift I'll come to accept.
In the cities of dreams my delicate arms
reach out toward the substantial,
to the place where they've all gone.
Goodbye.
Everything is like thin paper here.
Sometime, I'll see you all there.

Part Three:

Iridescent Where It Was

ABSENCE, LUMINESCENT

I

Arch inverted: white peony
and stamens, yellow. Center
of the body. Imagines.
Who is absent.

Fingers in my mouth—memory.
Dragonfly so blue in the head.
Orange, as fire, in the body.

Wings, transparence. Disappearing arms.

The space where he was. Aureole.
The space he is, she was.
And the opposite.

Defines the dragon which flies.
Iridescent where it was.
Echo of hued wings.

II

Heat at the center.
Heat where she was.
Lack of passion
where the torso
won't go. No path
through what is occupied.
Space.

III

Falls in a delicate arch, sees
own soul. Cadaver as shrine,
concavity.

So white. Says white flesh
and no spirit.

And touching the dead.
And touching what is not.

IV

In our calculations: the fact of matter
at lack of matter. The invisible, collapsed star.
If you must, a *black hole*. Thus the message of blackness
clearly indicating the coordinates of nothingness.

V

Remembers the pilgrimage
to the illumined wall.
And Christ's face
was said to appear.
God's face. Who sees it?
Child trying, trying.

Says to the child
(and it is the juncture)
go toward faith,
go through absence,
way to belief.

VI

(Not believing. Not seeing
and not believing. All the chants
to atmosphere, blanks.)

VII

Implodes, and all the way to nothing.
To illumine, first, then fades to black.
Hole where light was.
Absent star, perforation in there.

And memory of light, halo on.
Angels who walk among.
Seeming darkness around the head.

VIII

Falling languid. Lover not there.

IX

My sweet—the miles, the night.

*Darling my fingernails bear their half-
moons half-gone how long?*

*The house. Really my love.
The rooms are emptied. Haunted.*

Ghost of you come here body.

X

And I can see her, worshipper,

with a blue robe, biting her nails—
thinks *it's true, it's true,*
someone witnessed the miracles,
someone saw it all.

XI

And the mouths. Reeling the bass in.
Hooking the parabola of mouth, air.
Violence of fish body in the air.
Absence of water, presence of...

Open my mouth. His fingers going in.
The gills going open open nothing nothing.

Dragonfly so blue in the head.
On red wings, disappeared.

Sing sing going going.

XII

Of all the tendernesses at the end there was that bouquet of
wild orchids the constant ritual the washing the turning
of the body so cleansed by a lover's hands until the struggle
for breath the gasp and the body getting less warm the
ceremony and like the Egyptians all preparation then the
emerging presence the advent of absence the adornments
artifacts in the tombs where the lungs tighten in our awe
it's all there but spirit saying *goodbye are you gone it's*
difficult to tell you must be.

XIII

Theoretically, everything must be seen
as negative space. And then the task

of mistrust, tackled head on. There are limits
to the five, mortal senses. There are no limits
beyond.

They said.

XIV

Reunified through occupied
space. His fingers at my lips.

Explosion of black in the opened
mouth. Five fingers toward

the perforation, from dark
hair. Toward the void, toward
the presence in there.

Part Four:

Their Invisible Eyes

COASTAL

Toward what force on the beach
where the girl goes with fingernails
so white it hurts.

The sea is round, and moves in.
The clouds wax shadows, and wet.

Near thin waves at the edge
the girl feels such dizziness—
who is moving?

Away on a cliff there is a figure
so small it becomes a beacon
for the sea to swell to.

And a string could suspend them both
like two glassy beads above the surf.

Creatures emerge from the sand
and the sun remakes them.

The figure moves and breaks
the absolute stillness.
It's turbulent.

See the girl's white body half-
submerged, making a bridge
between elements. See the figure
meet sky meet earth.

How they rose, milleniums ago,

moving headlong—breathed
water, breathing air.

A tumult of creatures,
so much here, so much there.

PASTORALE

Now the turtle comes up from the pond, snapping,
   toward the pool where the goldfish are.
Are with their orange bodies sucking on algae.
   Where the couple doesn't swim but will,
in the pond, where the bass multiply
   and the canoe floats in the middle of the day.

Or to the flowerbed: iris, see lily, see marigold.
   With the dog poised for the yellow ball.
Cast over, the sky's all moving clouds
   like the wide net of vision.
And the stars with their invisible eyes.
   On the road with the trees so plentiful,
greens. Gone

back to the fine forms, manifold forms.
   There cabbage, there rhubarb, melon, bean,
neck, torso where the touch is, and they react.
   Where the body lets the light gather,
pushes it back. For the multiplicity
   of places where they'll respond, enact.
And the eyelashes pressed down, the wrists
   both tensed and loosed, the dimples
in the lower back.

Articulate—away from the straightness.
   From *meadow* to *insect-earthworm-weed-*
squirrel-wasp-rock. From linear
   to labyrinth. From axis to multus.
From the age-old to the half-heard, uttered.
   To the wandering off and back,
the pause. For silence   dispersal   echo.

For the juncture at which the day
moves forth and the tongue indulges
its mottled message.

GEODE

A woman pulling carrots
from the frozen earth
looks up. There,
on the perfect curve
of the planetarium
a few men patch and tar,
open their sacks
and lunch up there.
Imagine a spoon of stars
and night turned inside out.
A bitter carrot like a comet
on the tongue. She does.

*

At a silent performance:
dancers in black and red
with open mouths.
And sometimes, in the dark,
flashes of red and sound.
The human face white and round
and what if those who've never
spoken, spoke up now?

*

Watching the seismograph
a thousand miles from an earthquake
does some irreparable damage.
There are some things
we shouldn't think, can't take.
So we watch *The Creation of the Earth*

where homo sapiens appears
fifteen seconds from the end.
Little blotches on a green globe
just spinning.

★

The curve of the horizon
and white interior walls.
Which is to say,
a woman and a man
in a room of light,
and the earth supine
under a violet sky.
Is to say, the ceremony
of the body. A hand wanders
to a chip of wulfenite,
a mile away from the arrowhead,
dug up. To say,
I pull the clay up and out,
round and high
as I am.

★

Enormous canvas, invite us
into your cosmic scene—
exploding arcs, figures turning,
pillars of black painted green.
Famous geode, earthy aperture
begs us, says *walk in*.
Not even the frame prevents us.
Walk in. So we rocket
through the pigment once.
We're back on earth again.

INFINITE

What is octagonal: the city's silhouette,
my lover's lips in the dark, a rock.

It's almost eight.
How urban the sky is tonight
with its dust and brown light.
Silk pajamas on the neighbors
on the ninth floor next door.
I play the voyeur with my lamps out,
in silence. Chalking off the hours
by who walks where and when,
what I hear them say,
the times they touch.
Like a night in the cinema
after the numbers count down
to the first, enigmatic scene.

#

Of the two women, one is bold.
She walks from a tent in the mountains
with an empty cup, no shirt on.
Her body's hollows leave us
with numerical figures,
my lover and I,
eating the campfire's ashes
with the bread we made.
Imagining the inside of her mouth.

The stranger turns to me
and motions almost scientifically

to her wrist. It's exactly seven.
The sky is nearly yellow,
clouds like equations, women.

#

Probability takes the mathematician a long way.
Says: what will occur is a ratio
of what can and will occur.
Then laughs, ruffles the feathers
of his myna bird. Together
they purr in arithmeticals,
are earthward and lyrical.
Like the math man's kisses on me
later that night. Indiscriminate.
What we can't count.

CINEMA AUGUST

The theater is night
                while the sun   blazes
out on the pavement   where the
                                 light
            blinks/out

        to the screen & the actors
play secret/dramas with us   and isn't it

        our lives?   how we love it/so dark
with the body all eye/lit
                    up
& the distance
        we're immmersed   I come   alone

                they arrive
                in couples

we gather & sit   all shut up
                      usher it in

        then laugh/fear/offer tears
like thespians do   so directed

        yet genuine   with the world/called up
all myth & gift

        an evening with the analyst
        in the dark-haired stranger's bed
        dodging the blasts & bullets

with the possibilities   with a cup

of yellow popcorn

(later I'll say it wasn't good
            we'll say   she wasn't that good
                  it wasn't really probable)

                              but it's the afternoon/
      alone

everything is endurable   watch us line up
        for the prospect of goodness

It's my night/my seat's

                              in its own black
            bubble/here's the promise
some kind of fortune

                        no one can

            reach me now

COUNTRY OF BELIEF

"What better picture of believing could there be
than the human being who, with the expression
of belief, says 'I believe?'"
                                        —Wittgenstein

She says she loves him; she moves from the table
and places the flat of her hand on his chest.

What is unlocking itself? What measures the emotions
unlocked? Is it as far as she can go?

And who is distrustful—what has distrust
begotten in us? He believes her completely,

he must. (This is the image. It gets
at the first world inhabited by us.)

I'll write this in a state of utter believing.
I can write this in a century of disbelief.

Photographs of men at war. The masses in revolt.
A movie of the two in bed. The strangers at lunch.

Configurations of the face both unmasked, and masked.
Thought rising into flesh, to what end?

He reads her face in the fluorescence of a restaurant.
She offers him a happiness masked by despair.

And the picture gives its image for a minute.
And the photo shows the true nature of the soul.

On television, the soldiers declare their philosophies
for the cameras, for a worldwide audience.

And the director says *you must believe*
in the other, you must belie who you are.

And the scientist says: given the facts,
the evidence, the face on its collision course.

(It gets at the first world inhabited by us.)

Out in the fields where the people will go.
Out to the wild country places: expressiveness.

THE ANNUNCIATION

after the painting by Martini & Lemmi, quattrocento

It has been, and always will be
the way she leans back,
pulls her blue robe under her chin.
There is a golden shadow behind her:
halo, echo of another robe,
like a form she is about to take on.
She is the mother of Christ;
her book is closing upon her thumb.
It is hard for her to listen.

In the same way we are hesitant.
Delegations meet with the prospect
of peace but in separate rooms,
like couples with interminable
distances. They do not fear
the other's death like the lover
who waits for the next irregular breath
of she whom he loves. I am speaking,
for all I know, of listening.

Gabriel, on the left side of the painting,
utters his announcement.
Breath and sound become matter—
gold letters cross the panel:
room....atmosphere....lilies....
to the one who pulls away.

It is of course imaginable, predictable.
How is it possible for her to believe?
The ambassadors are witnesses
to a slide show, given everything
from the intricate filagrees of moss

to the round eyes of starving children,
from sea life to exploding stars.
It was obvious, the impossible
so real and obvious that this planet
and their allegiances, well,

I am out of breath.
Will breath become gold?
(And Mary will think *yes*.)
Will it move across.
(She will lean forward and dream *yes*.)
Something is trying to tell us,
waiting for us to take on
the brilliant shadow.
And if we would listen
(believing and saying *yes*)
who knows how the message
would become matter
then manifest itself.

FOSTER DIARY

8 June

Morning chant:
tigerlily—welts—origanum—
scratch—impatiens—bite—
where the sun alights.
And I'm rising out of bed
to sunlight, wounds, color.

10 June

These misshaped stones
foundations of old barns
Then the ghosts
with their chopping and dragging
Spirits gone into grass
float out of my head like water

12 June

In my sleep: a boy with the face of an angel
carves up a live bird. No squawks, no screams
for help. The farmers shake off their dreams,
go toward gardens with hoes all shine and gently.

21 June

Latches on the green doors
where thin blouses hang,
and the eastward breeze
through underwear,
windowscreens.

And everything's
attempting to get in—
flies, spiders, moths, toads.
And they do, and the few
boundaries. The faces
of gnats, their imprints
on our cheeks.

24 June

I wake with sheets twisted.
Next door, on white canvas,
two figures emerge
from cotton strips,
ash and hay.
Contortions and collage.
The nights like black brushes
do what they will.
Position me naturally,
after frenzy.

26 June

And the rectangles and arcs.
Rising out of the oven.
Floating out of the heat.
Open our mouths to nourishment.
Hovering like white moths
to lamps of wheat.

2 July

Fisherwoman by the pond gets
nibbles, a large bass, and two
too small get tossed back.
At night she reels in ivory

carp, an eel with a glass tongue,
and one all gold and onyx.
On the bank of her bed
she writhes into the blue light
of a rainstorm. She can breathe.

5 July

Pietá: girl with baby cat wrapped
in purple silk. And the tiny grave—
wildflowers, catnip, photos.
Handsful of soil going in.
The delicate configuration.
The garden tomb.

10 July

Bitter wasp now dangles from a tough web.
Watch the child creep over, grimace,
while the widow bites and sucks.
The hem of her dress is yellow.
It arrives like a halo.

15 July

Saying goodbye: death
of an infant robin.
Bales of hay, cut grass,
dandelions rooted
from the terrace.
Bittersweet pruned
all the way back.
Mulch of summer,
souls for the dreams
of novice farmers.

20 July

In the last days there was a horse in the heat
on her back, scratching. Sheep shifting and
honking. The sunset rippling in pools on a
dirt road. Going up the hill in the dark,
houses whitewashed in roses.

24 July

Watch:
she goes to the pond
and falls asleep,
head dripping.
An iris on the dam
ready to collapse.
A close-up,
then moving back
to an aerial view.
Minutiae then grandeur
till the end of summer
wakes her.

Foster, Rhode Island

INTO THE NEXT ONE

Eucalyptus, his mouth
on hers, on his. The taste.
The arch, the ankle—

the woman wearing a white sheet
and screaming, laughter.
She isn't a movie, a lover.
Is a loved woman forming a chasm
between her teeth. It's today
and what's important is the sheet,
brilliantly draped. It fell that way.

On a trip in Nevada there was a spot.
A trailer. A flower etched
against the desert. No time.
The heat and one flower, the desert.
It was the subject, it had to be,

and when a flower, a fuschia
so penetrating frightens me,
I remember.

Cotton, damask, like the husk
of some creature
where the body is implied.
I fossil-gather. Besides,
it's the end of the century,
the globe is warming,
forests are vanishing,
cultures are dying...

But the woman (I'd forgotten)
in the black chair, reeling.
The sheet exquisitely draped,
the blessed femurs
making their indentations.

Later, the body cloaking hers
for an hour.

What happens on this earth,
this time, next time, is implied.
Prophesied by these imprints
on our eyes. I'm thinking
of that flower in the desert,
shapes of carcasses and flowers
draped by the desert, thinking
gather your robes,
gather the wide robes my god
we're going there.

NOTES

"Savor, Harvest" and "The Annunciation" refer to the painting *The Annunciation* by Simone Martini and Lippo Memmi, 1333, in the Uffizi, Florence, Italy.

"Night of Fathers." The epigraph, from *The Egyptian Book of the Dead*, is spoken by the scribe Ani who calls back his body in the regions of the afterlife.

"Children of the Disappeared" refers to children kidnapped by officials of the military regime (in power until 1989) in Argentina. In what are now infamous events, political enemies of the state were commonly executed soon after being arrested. The exceptions were pregnant women. They were detained until just after giving birth, then executed with a bullet to the skull. Their children were "adopted" by generals in the military or other childless families friendly to the government. The ongoing process of identifying and finding these children has been undertaken by surviving families of the dead.

"Monstrous." Zozobra, or Old Man Gloom, is an ominous, 60 ft. tall puppet burned at the start of the annual Fiesta de Santa Fe, to ward off evil spirits for the celebration. As he wails, the flame dancer taunts Zozobra with burning torches, then sets him on fire.

"Tesoro" (spanish for *treasure*). The maiden is depicted in the painting *The Visitation* by "El maestro del retablo de los reyes catolicos" (master painter of the Catholic Kings of Spain), 15th century. It is housed at the University of Arizona Museum of Art, Tucson, Arizona.

"Country of Belief." The epigraph is from Wittgenstein's *Tractacus Logico-Philosophicus*.

Valerie Martínez has recently completed a volume of translations of Uruguay's Delmira Agustini (1886-1914). Her poems have appeared in numerous journals and anthologies and she has taught writing at the Universities of Arizona and New Mexico, as well as in rural Swaziland. She was assistant editor of *Reinventing the Enemy's Language*, an anthology of native women's writing (Norton, 1997). She is currently on the English faculty at New Mexico Highlands University.